A CAT'S guide

to being

purrrfectly cheeky!

Harwood J Smith

To every cat person

wherever you are in the world

who has innocently welcomed a cat into the household

clueless to the absolute chaos, mischief and

subsequent restructure of the family hierarchy

which followed

.... Hang in there!

Also, to my very own furry friend

who has kept me company on many long evenings

without whom

this book would have been completed a year earlier!

Humans......... what are they like to live with?

This is a question many cats ponder over! We're simply all compelled to learn more about these hairless, lanky wannabe companions of ours! The fact of the matter is every cat wants to know whether it's a worthwhile investment to take the plunge and adopt a human!

The modern human comes with a whole host of benefits: housing, heating, bedding, they clean up your poop too! Your stay will be full board and you can expect an exquisite range of crunchy biscuit hors d'oeuvres served throughout the day. Managing your human and their responsibilities is also rather simple and straight forward. The majority are completely oblivious to the dictator hidden behind our cute, fluffy exterior; thus, they're quickly trained to obey and serve!

So, why on earth wouldn't you want to adopt a human? Are there terms and conditions hidden away in the small print? The short answer is, yes! Although humans are largely considered safe, and as a way of life for many cats, there are one or two things you need to be wary of! Household guests such as little baby humans and dogs, late night curfews and annual trips to the vets are just a few concerns you may have. However, these are all dwarfed by the terrifying prospect of accidently adopting a *crazy cat person!*

This book is crammed with illustrations of everyday scenarios you can expect when living with a human. It's packed with useful advice and real-life stories. After reading this book, you will be purrrfectly equipped to make the right decision for you.

But be warned, under no circumstances should this book be shared with any humans! In the event that a human finds this book, it's likely they will become extremely needy as they discover how exceptionally adorable and hilarious, we are! Expect uncontrollable laughter, giggling and random snorting. Should they try and seek you out for extra cuddles, you must remember rule number 1: 'Humans may only spend time with us **on our terms and conditions!**' This is non-negotiable!

Now, before we delve any further, I'm off for a quick poo, and then I fancy a nap on the nice clean bed sheets ....

A brief history lesson.... *according to cats:*

Living alongside humans is nothing new. In fact, our ancestors can be traced back over 10,000 years helping humans survive. They needed a helping paw to point them in the right direction, and that's exactly what we did!

Perhaps the most well-known era was Ancient Egypt. The Ancient Egyptians were having a really tough time, they were being bullied by vermin! Gangs of rats would get together at bedtime and were stealing all their food supplies meaning many humans and baby humans were going hungry and malnourished! Being the kind, considerate, selfless species that we are, us cats couldn't just stand by and watch it all unfold in front of our big, beautiful eyes, oh no! We had no option but to heroically intervene!

We set-up squadrons and patrolled day and night catching every single rat who dared to trespass on the land. We taught the Ancient Egyptians how to hunt, how to protect their food and how to deal with rats. Their food supplies were soon replenished beyond their wildest dreams; however, they never quite got the hang of catching rats. Without us around the rats would soon return!

The Ancient Egyptians were well aware of this, and they begged us to stay with them. We accepted their offer, and it wasn't long before we were seen as gods, and rightly so! We were seen as the protectors from all things evil! Statues were built in our honour, etchings of us made in stone. We were fed delicious treats and given jewels in return for all the amazing work we did.

Word soon got around, and it wasn't long before humans all over the world wanted to live alongside cats. Humans just can't get enough of our amazing personalities and incredible skills. They needed a role-model, a species to idolise, and well, why look any further than cats!

"Waiter!

I don't like this brand anymore. Change it, change them all!"

"TO THIS VERY DAY IT'S IMPORTANT THAT WE NEVER EVER LET HUMANS FORGET THAT THEY WORSHIPPED US AS GODS IN ANCIENT TIMES!

AFTERALL......... WE CERTAINLY HAVEN'T FORGOTTEN!"

A quote from every cat that's ever existed

All homes come with your very own concierge who will assist you whilst you carefully consider whether to go outside or stay indoors, or go outside or stay indoors, or go outside or stay indoors! Life is so hard!

Movie nights are a great opportunity to bond with your humans!

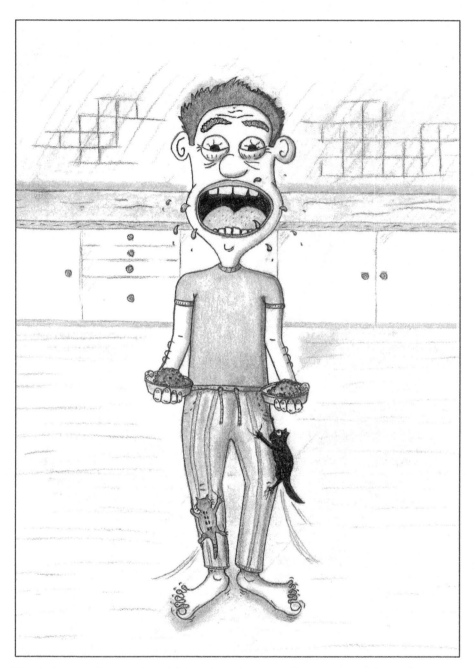

Training to hunt should begin when you're just a kitten!
Practice stalking your prey at mealtimes. Attack, when they
least expect it, give those claws a good workout!

Beware, all humans are masters of sorcery, it only takes a quick chin rub before you're in a trance with a goofy look on your face!

"Is this a convenient moment to mention that I can sense something rather strange in the corner by the ceiling?"

Nothing beats a good full-on stretch across the floor, are you watching me?

I'm just going to show you a bit of my belly, feel free to give it a scratch if you simply must!

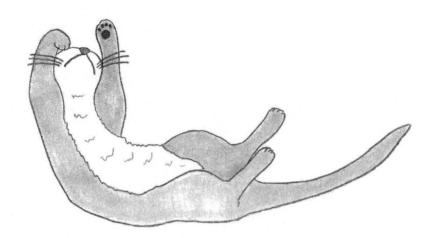

Have you ever seen anything this cute? I bet you can't resist giving me a tickle!

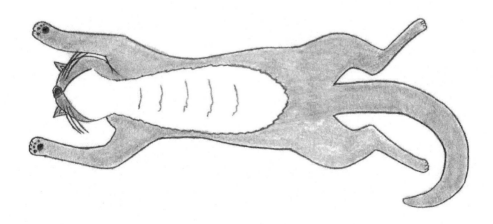

Okay, I can't make it any more obvious than this.... Will someone please, give me some attention!!

Remote working can become extremely stressful and it's important to remind your human to take a screen break every so often so that they can ~~give you lots of attention~~ rest their eyes and stretch their legs!

"Say **CHEESE**"

"My cat can hear me opening our fridge and taking a slice of ham out from the pack no matter where he is in the house! He magically appears expecting ham to be hand-fed to him! I now actually have to put my head inside the fridge and eat the ham to avoid him becoming suspicious!"

"My cat's idea of greeting me every morning and every evening when I return home from work is to act like he's excited to see me, whilst luring me to his empty food bowl the whole time. He then sits beside it and stares at me!"

"There was a period of several months when the usual brand of food we buy for our cat was out of stock everywhere. The only alternative available brands she would eat were extremely expensive! Luckily the shortages were soon over, and I stocked-up on all her favourites when I saw them available again in the supermarket. Unfortunately for us, our cat has decided that she will now only eat the extremely expensive brands. She will no longer eat the old brand! My shopping bill has increased substantially!"

"Our cat has a habit of letting out the most vile-smelling, silent pop-offs at the most inappropriate moments. He doesn't even flinch and looks completely comfortable and relaxed, the perfect crime! It has led to some very awkward conversations whilst hosting dinner friends and even an argument between my husband and I when my husband suggested maybe it wasn't the cat on one occasion!"

Cheeky cat story

Cat's name: Piglet *Cat's age:* 8 *Type:* Tortoiseshell *Human:* Jane

I'd joined my local neighbourhood watch group, and a couple down the road were hosting a gathering at their house one evening. I remember turning up and introducing myself, I hadn't spoken to the hosts before, I only really knew my immediate neighbours, so it was nice to get to know them and a few others who lived up and down the road. Their house was really cute, it felt very warm and cosy in the living room with a conservatory at the back which was open. It was then I noticed their cat spread-out asleep on one of the chairs in the conservatory, looking extremely comfortable I have to say!

It was a tortoiseshell just like my Piglet which was unusual I thought, I'd never seen it around outside before! I made my way over to have a closer look at their cat, it looked very similar to Piglet. In fact, it was almost identical! At this point the cat heard me approaching and opened its eyes. I immediately knew, it was Piglet! Her eyes opened very wide when she realised it was me staring right back at her, she couldn't believe she'd been caught, they looked like they were going to pop out of her head! She just froze. She was ever so still, almost like she thought she would be invisible if she didn't move!

I couldn't believe my cat was fast asleep on a chair in my neighbour's conservatory acting like she owned the place! Judging by how comfortable she was, it clearly wasn't the first time she'd been there!

I asked the host about the cat, and she told me that Piglet had been popping in for years here and there. She admitted she did offer her a bit of ham on occasions. This would explain Piglet's unaccountable weight-gain, and I'm pretty sure food was offered to Piglet more regularly than the lady let on. Afterall, I know how persuasive Piglet can be when it comes to food! I eventually told her that Piglet was my cat and we both had a laugh about the whole situation. Meanwhile Piglet must have sneaked out the door and was nowhere to be seen!

When I returned home later, who do you think was fast asleep on the sofa like nothing had just happened? Piglet! Cheeky cat!

[15]

Cheeky cat story

Cat's name: Ginger   *Cat's age:* 10   *Type:* Ginger   *Human:* Mary

Ginger is a rescue cat; we've had him since he was a year old. When he was around 7 years old, we started to notice he was developing hearing problems. He couldn't hear us calling him unless we were near him or in the same room, and even then, he struggled! When he was outside in the garden, particularly at night, sometimes we would call him for ages to try and get him to come indoors for the night to no avail. There were even a few occasions we thought he'd gone missing which is all a bit worrying especially when he may not be able to hear anything and be alert to the traffic and dangers all around!

Luckily, one of my best friends is a vet and we've been taking Ginger to her practice ever since we've had him. I called her up and explained to her about Ginger's hearing problem and she arranged to pop in on her way back from work the following day.

The next day when she arrived, we kept Ginger in the living room with us. She began by checking Ginger's ears which he did not like one bit! She then did several reaction tests by making various noises behind Ginger to see if he reacted, such as tearing paper, or knocking on a wall. Then she went into the hallway and closed the door and began making gentle knocking sounds and carried out a few other tests.

Well, I don't know whether it was because we had someone Ginger is not familiar with in our house, but Ginger seemed to react to all the tests, particularly when my friend left the living room which may be down to Ginger protecting his territory.

To cut a long story short, my friend advised me that Ginger has no hearing problems what-so-ever. It turns out that after several years of living with me and my family he has developed selective hearing! He just decides to ignore us unless it's in his best interest not to! I'm not really sure what to think about this, but we've got used to his ways now! He certainly hears okay when I'm serving up his dinner, the cheeky rascal!

Cheeky cat story

Cat's name: Unknown   *Cat's age:* Unknown   *Type:* Tabby   *Human:* Dorothy

This isn't actually a story about my own cat, it's just something I witnessed a few years back one sunny morning as I was doing some potting and planting in my front garden. I was just taking a break and having a nice cuppa in the sun enjoying the tranquillity when the moment was abruptly interrupted by a man yelling frantically! A scene was unfolding in front of my eyes as I watched George who lived in a bungalow a few doors down chasing a tabby cat which appeared to be holding a large fish in its mouth!

George must have been mid-70s and yet was running at a fair old rate, I was a little bit concerned as well as impressed! However, as athletic as George may have thought he was, unfortunately he was only ever going to come second in a race against a cat! The cat darted across the front lawn in my direction and in the-spur-of-the-moment I began clapping my hands loudly and hissing at it! The cat got spooked and dropped the fish on the grass and was gone in a flash!

George staggered over panting, and I got a bucket and filled it with water from the hose and picked up the slimy fish and popped it in! Once George stopped wheezing and had caught his breath, he explained that he had been doing some maintenance on his pond. He had taken off the mesh cover exposing the fish when his wife had called him in for a telephone call. He said he was indoors taking the call looking through the front window when he saw the cat jump over onto the front lawn with one of his fish in its mouth!

I'm pleased to say the fish was promptly returned to the pond and seemed unharmed by the ordeal and settled back in well.

Cheeky cat story (told from a cat's perspective)

Cat's name: Bubsy   *Cat's age:* 2   *Type:* Ginger   *Humans:* Greg & Emma

It was around 3am on a cold wet night and I'd just caught the biggest frog I'd ever seen in my garden! I just knew my humans would want to share the moment with me. I popped the frog in my mouth and ran through the cat flap into my house and trotted upstairs.

My humans sleep with their door open because they don't like me scratching it and meowing loudly at night when it's closed. I made my way into their room and jumped onto their bed and dropped the frog onto the covers between them. I could barely contain my excitement, I let out a series of quick meows and noises to wake my humans and I jumped about tapping the frog.

Mummy was the first to wake up. It took a few seconds for her eyes to adjust, and as she reached out to stroke me, the frog hopped, and I darted towards it to play. She was so impressed with what I'd caught she leapt out of bed and began running and jumping around frantically waving her arms and screaming loudly and uncontrollably at my daddy to wake up and see what I'd brought in!

Daddy woke up and switched on the light so he could take a better look at the big frog. By this time the frog had leapt onto the floor and as my daddy tried to catch it (he wasn't as fast as me) the frog hopped and wriggled underneath the bed. My daddy then had to get a torch and shine it under the bed to find the frog. It was turning into the best game ever, me and Daddy were stalking the big frog together whilst Mummy was almost hyperventilating with excitement as she stood on a chair in the corner of the room watching! She had tears of excitement running down her cheeks! We were all really enjoying ourselves!

Eventually Daddy coaxed the frog out with the end of a broom stick and put into a container. He then locked me in the room and took the frog back into the garden.

They didn't let me sleep with them that night. They locked their door and locked the cat flap to stop me going outside again. I spent the rest of the night scratching their door and meowing to let them know I was just outside their room and to remind them that it was nearly 4:30am, which is when I'd ideally like my breakfast! I think they were tired!

🐾 "It's amazing how heavy, awkward and completely floppy my cat becomes when you try to move him without his consent!"

🐾 *"My cat knows the exact minute his breakfast or dinner is due, and my word, does he make a fuss about it!"*

🐾 "My cat goes into the kitchen and drags his empty food bowl all the way into the living room where we're sitting and then keeps flipping it over with his paw to try and get his dinner served early. He does this a lot, he's so naughty!"

🐾 **"My cat greets me in bed every morning which is really sweet. She purrs the whole time, gives me little kisses with her little wet button nose, and gets so excited that she often begins to dribble! Sometimes as an encore, she will begin to choke on her own saliva right in front of my face as she dribbles and purrs, which is just lovely first thing in the morning!"**

🐾 *"I leave the doors around the house slightly ajar so my cat can enter and exit all the rooms as and when he pleases. Even though the gap I leave is sufficient; he always stands on two legs and gives the door an almighty shove until it's wide-open which is often followed by an unpleasant breeze of cold air! It can also become a bit scary if you're just settling down to a Saturday night horror movie with a glass of wine and your door appears to suddenly fling open on its own accord, only for a little face to appear a few moments later as he walks into the room looking very pleased with himself! He never shuts the door after him either!"*

Need a bit of alone time? Just sneak off and hide under the bed covers, your human will never find you! You'll be completely invisible!

"Dish me up a nice juicy leg please chef!"

Hacking up a hairball can be an inconvenience for both cats and their humans!

We're not nosey, it's just important to thoroughly inspect any new bags brought into the household!

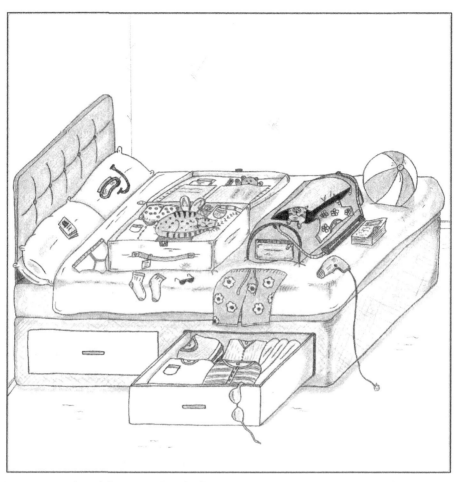

Luggage should never be left unattended! We're really not nosey…. honest!

I know how this looks, but we're absolutely, categorically, one hundred percent, **<u>NOT NOSEY!</u>** We're just passionate about neighbourhood watch!

"Well, this was a lovely surprise Pete, thank you very much for the tasty chunks of luxury ham, I enjoyed them very much! I'm just going to leave that last piece though because someone seems to have stuffed a worming tablet in it!"

"I'm just giving them a quick tickle……. Honest!!"

"Bring out the treats, then we can negotiate!"

Cats are always RIGHT! No matter what the circumstances are, never, ever, admit that you were wrong.... Even when your human must rescue you!

It's a known fact that cats have the cutest butts out of all the species in the whole world. There's never a bad moment to show off your butt. **If you got it, flaunt it!**

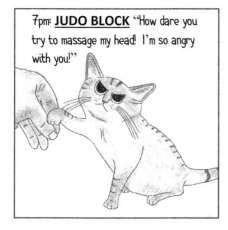

A cat demonstrating the correct way on how to use the new expensive scratch post that its human has lovingly purchased!

Dobby's Diary

A week in the life of Dobby

who resides in a house with his

retired humans

18 MONDAY

Pamper Day!

*Pick old claws

*Clean fur, remove any tufts

*Pick ears

*Clean butt

19 TUESDAY

WEATHER REPORT:

<u>100% CHANCE OF RAIN!!!!</u>

Stay in and nap all day. DO NOT GO OUT!

*Found piece of string on floor and eat it. Not sure that was the best idea I've ever had!!!!

20 WEDNESDAY

Burn of excess energy from having slept all day Tuesday by being extra needy! Follow Mummy around the house all day demanding attention!

** Note to self.... It appears that by being extra annoying today, Mummy has given-up and served me extra food and treats to keep me quiet! Remember this for future reference when hungry! **

<u>VET: 2PM</u>

Emergency appointment to see if vet can fully remove the piece of string I swallowed Tuesday night which is now dangling out of my butt!

<u>FULL MOON TONIGHT</u>

Relax all day and preserve energy in preparation

For my dramatic transformation into my alter ego

'MANIAC MOON CAT' as night falls and the full moon emerges!!!!

2AM – 2:30AM – Go crazy. See how many times I can hurtle up and down the staircase at full speed! Make as much noise as possible until humans are fully awake!

Spend the rest of the day eating and sleeping!

Grandchildren visiting: <u>VACATE HOUSE ALL DAY!</u>

"My cat will sit down right in front of me, or even rests against me whilst she casually proceeds to pick her claws really loudly, wash her butt, and even pick her ears! She also grunts as she does this! She has absolutely no shame!"

"My cat is capable of producing a poo in his litter tray which if left unattended could probably clear out a small town within an hour based on how bad it smells! He then proceeds to dig and scrape away in the litter for what seems like an eternity, just when you think he's finished covering it up, he starts digging all over again! Eventually he emerges looking very satisfied with himself. When I then go to clear his litter tray, I find litter all over the floor, against the side of the tray, even in other rooms where he has trodden it in. In fact, he's covered everything with litter apart from his actual poo!"

"My cat is quite heavy, and she doesn't seem to realise when she walks over me her weight-to-paw ratio can actually be quite painful depending on where she stands!!!!"

"I never realised just how nosey cats are. Our cat must be right in the middle of anything and everything that happens around the home."

"My cat has a habit of clawing our carpet or sofa when he demands attention. He's worked out that this method always works without fail because it prompts me to react immediately!"

Cheeky cat story

Cat's name: Catzilla *Cat's age:* 4 *Type:* Tabby *Human:* Mandy

Catzilla is a rather large tabby, he's a bit on the chubby side I must admit! I was just settling down to lunch one afternoon when he came in from the garden looking very shaken-up! He had a worried look on his face and I just knew something wasn't quite right! It was then that I noticed a grey gloopy like substance which was covering all his big paws. He was licking and biting at them furiously to no avail, I could see he was getting really frustrated and did not like the taste!

Like any good cat mummy, I took Catzilla to the bathroom and began washing his paws with a gentle warm shower in the bathtub. This was much harder than it sounds on paper, he's incredibly strong when he wants to be and not a fan of water! But he's a good boy and knows not to scratch or bite, and I think he knew I was helping him anyway. Half-an-hour later I had managed to remove all the thick substance from Catzilla's paws although I could not fathom out quite what it was!

Catzilla soon dried-off and was back to his usual self and I decided that I would lock him in for the rest of the day just to keep him out of mischief. It was around 4pm when I heard my son coming in from school. He was chuckling away as he began excitedly explaining that our neighbour was outside with some workmen looking at a stretch of path leading up to his front door. My son explained that the path was being re-done and concreted over earlier in the morning when he had left for school. Apparently, there were now a set of paw prints in the actual path which had hardened!

I took a sneaky look out from the upstairs window and could see my neighbour, hands on hips looking at his garden path which did indeed have indentations of several large paw prints and blotches going across it. He was looking a little agitated as he chatted with the workmen! I'm so thankful that several other cats also live down our road, hopefully he will never find out who the guilty party was! I do hope he never notices how big Catzilla's paws are though!

[37]

Cheeky cat story

Cat's name: Sylvester   *Cat's age:* 5   *Type:* Black & White   *Human:* Heather

I've had Sylvester since he was a kitten. He's extremely cheeky and a very outdoorsy cat, all the neighbours know Sylvester!

It was a Saturday and I remember giving Sylvester his breakfast. Afterwards he went out in the garden through his cat-flap as usual. Then I went off to visit my mum for the day with my husband and our 12-week-old baby. We returned home in the evening and I served-up Sylvester's dinner and called out to him expecting him to come bursting through the cat-flap, but he didn't! Time went on, and soon it was late into the night and there was no sign of Sylvester!

It got to two days and Sylvester hadn't returned. I printed-out missing cat signs and pinned them up all around the local area. Sylvester has a very distinctive white spot on his nose, so I was hoping he would be easily recognisable if I highlighted this in the posters.

Days turned to weeks, and weeks turned to months and Sylvester still hadn't been found. I had given up hope at this point and had removed all the posters, I was so upset, I really missed him!

Life continued, and I remember getting back from our friends one Friday evening. This would have been around five months since Sylvester went missing. We opened the front door, took off our shoes, walked into the living room, and there on the sofa was Sylvester! He was as large as life and just looking at us like nothing had happened! I almost fainted! He must have come in through the cat-flap (I had kept it unlocked ever since he went missing hoping for a miracle).

Well, after the initial shock, Sylvester jumped down from the sofa and began purring, dribbling, and rubbing his body against our legs, not to mention giving each of us several head-butts! I gave him loads of hugs; I think he had missed us so much. He wouldn't leave us alone; I'd never heard him purr so loudly!

[38]

I sent my tired husband out to the 24-Hour supermarket to get loads of cat food and treats because I had given the old stuff away. Sylvester certainly got treated to a banquet of food that night!

Well, the story gets even stranger at this point. I had taken Sylvester to the vets for a check-up to make sure he was okay after going missing for so long. His health was fine, no malnourishment or weight loss or anything, the vet implied that he must have been getting food from somewhere!

By now a week had passed since Sylvester had returned and I remember walking to the high street to run a few errands one weekend. I was walking down a back road about two or three miles from home when I came across a missing cat sign, and I just couldn't believe it; the cat in the photo was Sylvester! I recognised his markings. I had to do a double-take and check it wasn't one of the old signs I had put up previously and forgotten to take down, but it wasn't, and anyhow this was a bit far out from our house!

I called the number and got chatting to an elderly lady who explained Sylvester turned up a while back and had been living with her since, she assumed he was a stray as he'd been sleeping under a bush in her garden for a week before she took him in! The lady was grateful that I let her know Sylvester was safe and she was very apologetic. I do think she had grown attached to him over the short time he had been living with her. I can look back and laugh now, however I still can't believe my Sylvester just left us for five months and then came back and acted as if nothing unusual had happened.

My husband and I tried to piece together what we think had happened and we believe it may be due to us having had our first baby at the time. We think Sylvester got a bit jealous and ventured a bit too far out, got lost and couldn't find his way home!

I'm pleased to say a couple of years have passed since and we've had no more incidents. If anything, Sylvester stays home a lot more often now and likes lots of attention! I think he genuinely gave himself a fright back then when he got completely lost!

Sylvester's version of events: "I wasn't lost, I was kidnapped by an old lady who lured me into her home with a slice of ham and a saucer of milk!"

HOW IT STARTED

VS

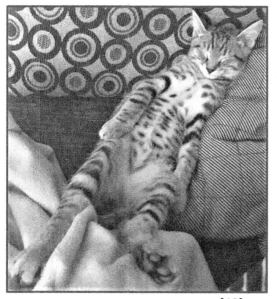

HOW IT'S GOING!

[40]

Cheeky cat story (told from a cat's perspective)

Cat's name: Mojo   *Cat's age:* 7 Months   *Type:* Black & White
Humans: Paul, Kerry & Lauren

Recently I found the best hiding place EVER! It was so amazing! I was out in the garden one morning and I noticed a gap in-between the garage on the side of our house and the wall on our neighbour's house. It was just big enough to squeeze myself into! Well, this was my chance to really impress my humans with my expert hiding skills. I couldn't wait!

I began forcing my way through the tight gap until I was completely wedged in and couldn't move any further. Then I just waited to see how long it would be before my humans found me! Well, the minutes and hours passed, and I could hear my humans calling, but they still couldn't find me! Eventually I decided to give them a clue as to where I was and began meowing loudly. It was my 10-year-old human who found me first, and she immediately called the adult humans and began to cry uncontrollably saying I was stuck, and that she'd never see me again!

Mummy took her inside whilst Daddy began to swear to himself and grumble a lot after shining a torch down into the gap where he could see my butt facing him! I think he was grumpy because he lost the game of hide and seek by not finding me first!

Daddy reversed the car out of the garage and got his building tools out. He began hammering and chiselling away at the garage wall from inside to remove the bricks around the area where I was wedged in. He did this very carefully and it took him quite a long time. Mummy came out to join us and eventually there was a hole in the wall big enough for Daddy to put his arm under me and help me squeeze through into the garage. I walked straight past Daddy because he was quite sweaty and smelly at this stage, I ran to Mummy, and she gave me a big hug!

It was now quite late, Mummy took me into the warm house and rewarded me with the biggest plate of my favourite food, chicken in jelly and biscuits! It was so yummy! We left Daddy in the cold garage on his own to put the house back together!

[41]

Cheeky cat story

Cat's name: Scooby   *Cat's age:* 7   *Type:* Black   *Human:* Jill

I still get embarrassed when I think back to this occasion! Our neighbours opposite were hosting a barbeque at the weekend and had invited everyone nearby. Only having moved in a few months back, we were a bit nervous, but my husband and I thought it would be fun meeting everyone. Our two children were also invited, it would be a good opportunity for them to make friends.

Saturday came around and we all headed over to our neighbours, it wasn't long before we were mingling, eating, having one or two drinks in the garden, and having a good time. The day was going really well up until the moment a cat darted out from the open backdoor with a massive raw beef burger in its mouth quickly followed by an angry host shooing it away! It just had to be our cat Scooby, didn't it!

I quickly made up my mind not to mention it was our cat! I just joined in with all the other adults who were laughing, shaking their heads, and tutting at the naughty cat as we watched Scooby make his way over the fence with his takeaway burger! Scooby's very fast, so I was hoping nobody got a good look at him!

That lasted about two seconds before my son blurted out **'MUM IT'S SCOOBY!'** Obviously, the only way to avoid humiliation at this stage was to pretend I was short-sighted as I began to apologise for Scooby's behaviour after taking in this brand-new information that my son had just kindly shouted out to everyone in about a half-mile proximity! Thankfully my neighbours all found this rather hilarious, with the host insisting they'd send Scooby an invite next time! The things our cats put us through!

"You have three seconds to sense that I no longer want my belly tickled before your arm resembles something reminiscent to that of a shark attack!"

"You snooze, you lose! I didn't intentionally steal your nice warm seat the moment you popped to the kitchen…. Honest!"

"I just want to see what happens if I gently tap this glass towards the edge of the unit! The suspense is thrilling!"

[45]

It's polite on occasions to greet your human with a cracking headbutt! Don't worry, be as rough as you like, we're fairly certain their heads are designed for this!

"Now, the man in the pet shop said this expensive fountain would definitely encourage you to drink more fresh water!"

.... 5 minutes later in the garden!

Stealth-mode activated!

Treat your human to a gift from time to time, they love a good surprise!

It's mandatory to have a poo the very moment your human has just finished cleaning and changing the litter in your tray!

ARE YOU LIVING WITH...

A CRAZY CAT PERSON!!!!

Definition of a crazy cat person: A human usually residing with multiple felines who would happily live in a world populated entirely of cats! Usually identifiable by the tufts of cat fur stuck to their attire, particularly during the shedding season. Conversations normally start with the words 'my cat...!' Friends, family, and colleagues will be given mandatory lectures where they will be taught each cat's name, appearance, and personality before having to endure countless stories about them! Finally, there's a high probability of random cat photos or video's being sent day or night to the mobile phones of anyone who knows a crazy cat person!

The following survey is a useful tool to calculate just how obsessed with cats, your human is! It's recommended they complete the survey being as honest as possible!

1) Do you own any of the following items. Award (1) point for each item you own.

- A coffee mug featuring cats
- A cooking apron featuring cats
- A tea towel featuring cats
- A food tray featuring cats
- A pair of oven gloves featuring cats
- Any ornaments of cats which are on display around the home
- Slippers featuring cats
- Pyjamas featuring cats
- A cat calendar
- **A hilarious book about cats** ✓
- A cat teddy
- Socks featuring cats
- Jewellery or charms featuring cats
- A jigsaw puzzle featuring cats
- Coasters or table mats featuring cats
- A doormat featuring cats

2) Have you ever given a card or a gift to your cat on special occasions, for example on birthdays or Christmas? (5 points)
3) Have you given your cat a nickname besides their actual name? (3 points)
4) Do you put on a silly voice that is only used when you talk to your cat? (3 points)

5) Do you have a screensaver of your cat on your phone, laptop, or any apps? (5 points)
6) Have you ever taken your cat for a walk on a leash? (10 points)
7) Do you clip your cat's claws? (8 points)
8) Does your cat wear a fancy collar or one with its name on it? (7 points)
9) Are you subscribed to an online cat forum or club? (10 points)
10) Are you obsessed with videos of cats on YouTube? (5 points)
11) Do you ever give your cat a bath? (10 points)
12) How many cats do you live with? (1 point for each cat)

....

RESULTS BELOW

(WARNING, NOT TO BE DISCLOSED TO YOUR HUMAN)

0-9 points: Your human is considered safe and normal

10 – 19 points: Caution, your human is on their way to becoming a crazy cat person without realising!

20 – 29 points: Your human is officially a crazy cat person! It's recommended you try observing their behaviour daily! Just about bearable!

30 – 39 points: WOW!!!! Your human is well and truly obsessed with cats! Begin planning emergency escape route should you ever need some alone time for when they become clingy and demand your attention!

40 – 49 points: LEAVE NOW! Calmly walk to the nearest exit and vacate the property. It's only going to get worse from here, it's likely your human has started to believe they're some form of cat! They'll be eating your food and using your litter tray before long!

50+ points: We're speechless!!!! This has never happened! Good luck to any cat whose human has just scored 50+ points! Truth is, you could fly to the moon, and they'd still track you down! Follow previous instruction immediately! Report your human to the local animal centre, they officially believe they're a cat! They may need to be re-homed!

What your name tells us about your human:

- You're named after flowers or nature. Examples include, *Poppy, Sunflower, Meadow, Bluebell.*

Your human is likely to be a very cheerful person, a bit simple, and amazed by everything! They're often confused!

- You're named after a character in a children's movie or show. Examples include, *Simba, Baloo, Nemo, Olaf, Buddy, Pikachu.*

Hopefully a child has picked your name, otherwise it means your human is a full-grown baby!

- You're named after a move character. Examples include, *Godzilla, Kong, Rambo, Mystique, Chewbacca, Groot.*

Your human believes they are unique and quirky. They have a false sense of coolness about themselves when they are very much **not!**

- Your name is associated with a computer game. Examples include, *Sonic, Mario, Zelda, Tetris, Bowser, Blanka, Tails.*

GEEK ALERT!!

- You have a human name. Examples include, *Gary, Dave, Denzil, Clive, Emma, Jenny, Cindy.*

Possible crazy cat person! This is not normal behaviour, extreme caution recommended until you're certain your human can be trusted!

- You're named after food. Examples include, *Peanut, Chilli, Porkpie, Haribo, Chopstick, Popcorn, Dumpling.*

It's likely your human is a secret eater and may require an intervention!

- You're named after an alcoholic drink. Examples include, *Whisky, Brandy, Sherry, Tequila, Bailey, Mojito.*

Your human may like a beverage or two! It's quite possible they were in a pub when they thought of your name!

 Cats at Christmas

"Ah…. I'm glad you're back from work Trevor, the Christmas tree seems to have fallen over again!"

Cats at Christmas

Locate the human who emits the most body heat during winter but be prepared for fierce competition!

🧦 A Christmas cat story 🌿

Cat's name: Casper   *Cat's age:* 4   *Type:* Black & White   *Human:* Sue

It was Christmas day, and we'd travelled up to my parent's house. The journey was over three hours, and we were staying over. We'd just finished our big turkey dinner when my husband received a call from our neighbour. Our burglar alarm had been triggered back at our house! Our neighbour had a spare key but was reluctant to check it out in case somebody was inside.

We decided the quickest solution was to contact our local police station and see if an officer could attend the property using the spare key our neighbour had. We were all very worried, our alarm had never been triggered before, especially with-it being Christmas!

My youngest son was crying because he was worried about our cat! Casper was locked in the living room with access only to the kitchen and dining area. All other doors were shut off because of the burglar alarm system. The way the system works is that each outside door and window is fitted with a sensor which triggers the alarm if opened whilst the alarm is set. Our hallway also has a motion detector.

I then remembered we had the pet camera in the living room which was linked to my smart phone. You can access it and view your home live and move the camera around, it has a very wide lens as well to cover a large area. It also records any movement detected which you can view later (a way of checking what your pet has been up to). As I accessed the live camera, we immediately noticed the living room door was open! I then viewed all the recorded motion detection footage, and I couldn't quite believe what I found!

I was watching footage of Casper standing on two legs against the living room door and pulling at the handle with his paw until the door eventually opened. As soon as he entered the hallway, the alarm sounded, and he dashed off! Casper was our Christmas burglar! A story which was quite difficult for my husband to explain to the police officer already on the way to our house!

We've since had all our door handles replaced with round knobs to avoid any future mishaps!

"Thanks for my new bed, it's just perfect!"

 Cats at Christmas

At family gatherings, seek out the human who looks most likely to sneak you a bit of food! <u>Top tip</u>: It's usually the innocent looking little grandma!

Cats at Christmas

Cat 1: "Should we warn the humans about the chubby bloke climbing through the window?"

Cat 2: "Nah, as long as they're still alive to serve our breakfast come morning, it won't really affect us!"

"Don't mind me, I'm just taking a quick shortcut across you because I can't be bothered to walk around you!"

"MUST CATCH FLY! NOTHING ELSE MATTERS!"

What every cat believes they look like when they arch their back and puff out their tail!

IT ALWAYS FEELS LIKE, SOMEBODY'S........

WATCHING ME!!!!

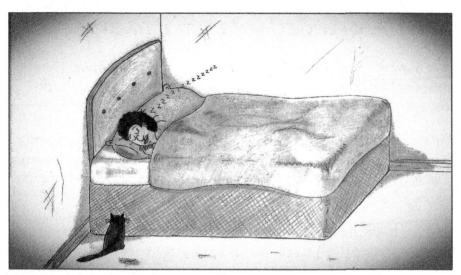

IT ALWAYS FEELS LIKE, SOMEBODY'S........
WATCHING ME!!!!

The dreaded vets, what to expect!

First things first, a brutal duel is about to commence between you and your human as they use all their strength and might to try and force you into a tiny cage! If they succeed, you're off to the vets!

If it's your first visit, be prepared to have a microchip wedged under your skin so that your every movement can be tracked by the animal police, there's no escape! Then, without any warning a thermometer is shoved in your butt to check your temperature!

Next, your weight is taken, and don't expect any sympathy if the vet happens to find that you're carrying a few extra pounds, oh no! They'll openly announce that you're morbidly obese and need to go on a diet! They'll even give your human a lecture about rationing your food!

Whoops, I nearly forgot to mention the massive jab that gets plunged into the soft tissue surrounding your neck! All in all, a lovely day out!

After your health check is completed, strangely your tiny cage is much more appealing, and you will happily go back inside! You then have to wait in reception with all the other sick animals whilst your human takes out a small loan to cover the bill!

But wait, there's more.........

Should the vet have determined that you require a prescription, you'll need to wait even longer! Eventually, an overly chatty receptionist with an unnecessarily loud voice will announce to the world that your worming tablets are ready for collection! How utterly embarrassing!

As soon as you're back home, it's mandatory to run away and hide from your human for the rest of the day or even the rest of the week on some occasions! Make no eye contact with anyone, and thoroughly milk the situation to score lots of sympathy and treats!

"What's the matter? Did you forget how freakishly strong I become when the cage comes out?"

"It turns out that our cat actually hadn't been spayed! We found out the hard way!"

"By sheer coincidence (**or not**) our Ragdoll cat becomes exceptionally vocal, clingy, and a right nuisance when I'm in the middle of a work video conference from home! She's so blatant, she simply doesn't like me diverting my attention to anyone else when she's around!"

"My cat taps me with her paw or gently puts her teeth around my finger to signal she wants attention and chin-rubs! She does this about ten times a day!"

"Every summer our cat partakes in one of his favourite hobbies in the garden, knocking the rose heads off from my lovely rose bushes as soon as they bloom! For some reason he's obsessed with them. He then plays with them for a few minutes before getting bored and doing something else!"

"My cat eats his own claws! He picks at them, and then eats any that he pulls out. It's disgusting!"

"Our cat goes around sniffing and eating any little bits he finds on the floor, particularly in the kitchen! He makes a sound which is a cross between a purr and a snort resembling the noise a vacuum cleaner makes!"

"My cat walks into the living room around 10pm every night and dramatically flops down making himself as flat as possible and rests his little chin on the ground looking up at me with big eyes and a little sad mouth like he has the whole world on his shoulders! Sometimes he even makes little sad noises for maximum effect whilst staring into my eyes the whole time. He's doing this because he wants more food! We then have a silent stand-off for about ten minutes before I usually give in and serve him a little portion of food! When he hears me getting his bowl, miraculously, he's suddenly extremely happy, bouncing about all over the place and full of life again! He eats the food and then casually strolls off to bed!"

"Our cat is the messiest eater ever, bits of food end up stuck to the wall, on the floor away from his mat, stuck to the outside of his dish, everywhere! He even scoops his food up with his paw on occasions and licks it off, not great when it's a gravy dish! It's not unusual to see him with a bit of food stuck to his face that he's missed, he's so messy!"

"My cat prepares for breakfast and dinner an hour earlier than it's due every day! He pesters me non-stop until it's served!"

"Every year when the clocks go back, my cat never accepts the fact that his breakfast and dinner times have changed!"

"My cat is obsessed with me when I use the bathroom. He waits outside the door every morning until I come out!"

"I'm a firm believer that cats have mastered the art of teleportation. I see my cat leave the room, next minute he's behind me just staring. I genuinely don't know how he got there! He just appears everywhere without making a sound. I'm constantly tripping over him!"

[69]

Cheeky cat story

Cat's name: Buster   *Cat's age:* 5   *Type:* Ginger   *Humans:* Sarah & Will

My boyfriend had just purchased a very expensive flat screen TV with surround-sound! He was fiddling about with it and decided to play a video on YouTube which was made for cats! You can probably guess where this is going already!

The video was of a bird feeder where lots of different birds fly in and out pecking at the seeds, chirping, and flapping the whole time, a few squirrels too! The surround sound made it seem like they were in our living room with us! It wasn't long before Buster, our ginger tom cat appeared! He was very interested in the show as you can imagine!

He began making lots of little noises and sounds which cats tend to do when they're birdwatching. There was one particular large grey bird that really seemed to agitate Buster! Every time it appeared, he became very vocal and restless!

It eventually all got too much for Buster, he couldn't contain his excitement anymore and he darted towards the television in full pounce mode! He leapt up and gave the screen several quick whacks with his paw! Before me or my boyfriend could react, Buster's primal instincts got the better of him and he just launched himself against the television!

Now I should explain, being a ginger tom cat, he's a big solid cat! He weighs a tonne! When you also take into consideration modern televisions are very light weight and slim, there's only really one way this whole scenario was going to play out!

The television toppled back against the wall before falling flat on its back and sliding off the stand making a huge thud as it hit the wooden floor! Buster ran-off out of the living room in a flash. The sound of birds chirping fizzled out and the screen was ruined!

Relations were a bit frosty for a few days, but I'm happy to say that Buster and my boyfriend have made-up, and we can look back and laugh at the situation, well I can at least!

Cheeky cat story

Cat's name: Kit-Kat   *Cat's age:* 5   *Type:* Black   *Humans:* Agatha & Winston

I remember hanging the washing out in the garden and I could hear Kit-Kat meowing but couldn't work out where from. I looked around the garden everywhere before I eventually located him, to my absolute horror, Kit-Kat was up on the roof of the house next to the chimney!

I called my husband to decide whether we needed to call the fire brigade or not to get him down. My husband decided he could deal with the situation, and he went and fetched the ladder from the garage along with the cat-carrier.

We rested the ladder against the edge of the roof for a while to see whether Kit-Kat would make his own way down, but he didn't budge. So, my husband decided to climb up the ladder with the cat carrier and some treats to try and entice Kit-Kat down towards him. Again, Kit-Kat wasn't interested.

Finally, my husband began climbing onto the actual roof on all fours, slowly making his way towards Kit-Kat. He had the cat carrier with him. To say I was extremely worried at this point was an understatement! I told my husband to come down and we could call the fire brigade, but he didn't listen!

My husband was getting closer to Kit-Kat, he grabbed the chimney to balance himself and then tried to position the cat-carrier in the hope Kit-Kat would go into it. Kit-Kat didn't like this idea, and he began walking further away and started to make his way to the other side of the roof around the front of the house!

I rushed around to the front garden worrying that Kit-Kat would fall, but he just calmly walked across to the neighbour's side of the roof, then he moved down to the lower part, jumped down onto our neighbour's porch roof with no trouble at all, then from the porch roof he jumped onto the lower connecting wall and then simply jumped down onto the front lawn.

Meanwhile my husband was now stuck on the roof and realising it was a lot harder to climb down than it was to climb up! I eventually had to call the fire brigade to come and rescue him!

[71]

Cheeky cat story

Cat's name: Wolverine *Cat's age:* 2 *Type:* Tabby *Human:* Olly

It's partly my own fault for participating in a game that just naturally developed between me and my cat from when he was just a kitten! He's now two years old and is showing no sign of getting bored!

The game is quite simple, Wolverine enjoys nothing more than to hide somewhere and then jump out and scare me! He gets himself into a crouching down position, his little butt moves from side-to-side as he gets ready to pounce, and then he jumps out and even does a little mini roar like a Lion, just a lot more quieter and squeaky sounding! He gives me a quick tap with his fuzzy little paw, I then react like I'm scared, and he trots off happy as anything waiting to do it all over again!

Now I should add, this is all very well when we're both playing, because I'm anticipating him jumping out at me, and I know where he's hiding! However, he's now started to randomly play this game when I'm actually not expecting it at all!

One occasion was when I was working on my laptop, I had a hot coffee in my hand. I was completely unaware that Wolverine had crept up behind my chair. Next thing I feel two little paws grab my arm very quickly accompanied with a mini roar. I was so shocked, I jumped out of my chair, my coffee went flying all over my arm and laptop, I cracked my toe so hard against the leg on my desk that I broke the bone, and my pulse reached the level of an Olympic sprinter! I was not impressed one bit!

The next day at work was great fun trying to explain to my colleagues why I was walking with a limp as well as having my arm bandaged up! I genuinely think a few of them thought I had been in a fight, I guess it's quite hard to believe the mischief a cat can cause unless of course you have a cat!

Nothing has changed since, Wolverine still loves to hide and scare me, I just ensure I'm extra careful and alert when drinking coffee. I genuinely believe he thinks I'm another cat, because it's the kind of game you often see two cats play together!

"There's always room for a little one, you'll barely notice I'm here!"

If you require urgent attention, simply tap your human to activate!

"Just be patient, letting you out of the bathroom is the next item on my agenda!"

We're still no closer to explaining why all humans become obsessed when we accidently leave our tongue sticking out! Trust us, your human is too!

"Morning.... we heard your partner left you about a month ago!
Guess you're probably thinking of getting a few cats soon?"

Pretending to express affection towards your human with a little wet nose kiss is the perfect opportunity to wipe away any lingering boogers! The best part is, they'll think you're super cute as you're doing it!

"I'm just going to eat this bit of grass so that I can go indoors and dramatically throw-up everywhere!"

Ask Angus, all your problems solved:

Dear Angus,

I fell asleep on the sofa with my tongue hanging out, snoring, and with my legs sticking up in the air. When I awoke, I accidentally rolled of the sofa! Unbeknown to me, my evil human was filming the whole ordeal on her phone because she thought I looked cute! The video has now gone viral on YouTube, everyone is laughing at me! What should I do?
Cookie, age 4

Dear Cookie,

Since when did cats start caring what humans think or do? They're completely inferior, it's not worth worrying about!

Dear Angus,

Lately I've become concerned that I can't poo! I go to my litter tray as normal; I dig a hole, squat, and do what feels like a massive poo! However, when I go back to check moments later, it's vanished, there's nothing there! Did I actually do a poo or was it just a figment of my imagination? Please help!
Beefy, age 7

Dear Beefy,

It's more than likely that your human immediately disposes of your poo! I suspect this is because it's extremely smelly and nobody wants it wafting around the home! In other words, you smell! I hope this has put your mind at rest and cheered you up!

Dear Angus,

Every August for the last four years my human goes through a dramatic transformation for two weeks! I barely see him apart from breakfast or dinner time. When he does show-up, he looks like a woman, is shorter in height and has developed a high-pitched voice! I get very frightened, and I hide!
Tiddles, age 5

Dear Tiddles,

It sounds like your human is simply taking a summer vacation and has hired a cat-sitter to feed you! I suggest you stop panicking!

Dear Angus,

My human often wakes me up by shaking me just after I've fallen into a deep sleep. I awake to find her staring at me all wide-eyed and asking if I'm okay in a silly voice! Why is she behaving like this?   Dasher, age 3

Dear Dasher,

It's likely that you're entering the 'rapid eye movement' (REM) phase of sleep. Cats are well known for this, and it's completely normal, healthy in fact! It's a sign of deep sleep or that you're dreaming! However, what you will be unaware of is the fact that your eyes will be rolling around, even opening, your bottom lip quivers revealing all your teeth, your whiskers will be twitching, and your legs are probably kicking out, not to mention all the weird noises! It basically looks like you're being possessed! To put it bluntly, your human is waking you up because you're scaring the living daylights out of her!

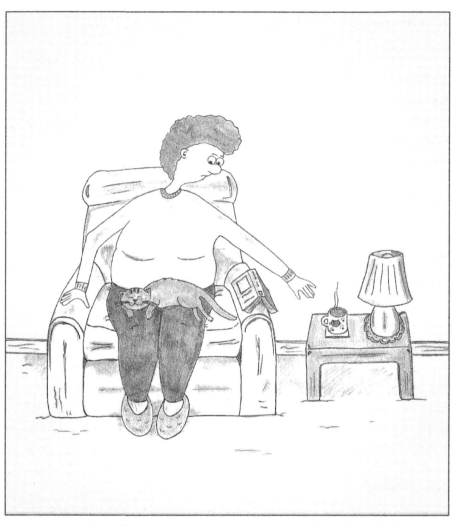

Humans are legally obligated to remain perfectly still for the entire duration of a cat-lap-nap!

About once a week, without any warning, your human will suddenly turn into a cleaning-crazed, erratic, zigzagging, vacuuming monster! RUN! HIDE! GET OUT! **DON'T LET THE VACCUM GET YOU!**

"Oh…. I didn't realise you were behind me! Erm…. I'm just carrying out a quick risk-assessment on these new curtains!"

"Er……… It's 5:30pm, my usual dinner time, and I can't help but notice my bowl is empty!"

"It's now 5:32pm, **QUIT MESSING WITH ME AND FETCH MY DINNER!**"

"I got a bit carried away with this new textured wallpaper. Sorry! Can we get some more?"

"Do you remember when I was a kitten and you used to play that game with me where you wriggled your toes under the bed sheets? Because I do........."

The carpet can be used as a giant toilet roll as and when required. A quick scoot can remove even the most stubborn of stains!

"You know the rules, I only open the door myself when you're not around! Now up you get!"

"**WAKEY WAKEY SLEEPY HEAD**, my breakfast isn't going to make itself!"

"You carry on, don't mind me!"

Cyprus, Greece, Turkey, these are just a few of the exotic locations humans travel to for a romantic break, and the opportunity to be serenaded by cats in the local restaurants in return for half their food!

CAT CONFESSIONS

"*Turns out that the children's sandpit next door is not a luxury litter tray!*"   *Twinky, age 7*

"Last Christmas I got caught nibbling on Daddy's turkey leg which had been left on the kitchen counter to cool down. Mummy still served it up to Daddy and he eat it all! We've never told him the truth!"   *Noddy, age 9*

"**Chewing Mummy's Michael Kors handbag is not the same thing as chewing on an old shopping bag!**"   *Coco, age 2*

"**I just wanted to sniff a wasp to see what it smelt like....**"
Speedy, age 4

CAT CONFESSIONS

"I accidentally knocked Mummy's cup of tea off the bedside table....... Oh, and I forgot to mention it spilt over an electrical adaptor socket causing the fuse-box for the whole house to trip!"
Oscar, age 16

"I was caught on our motion sensor pet camera opening the refrigerator door and helping myself to left over chicken when my humans were away for the night. I also didn't close the door, so all the food had to be replaced when they returned home the following day!"
Maximus, age 5

"My human left his laptop open when he went to the toilet. Before he left, there was a half-finished report he was working on. When he returned, it was gone, and I was sitting on the keyboard!"
Jellybean, age 9

"My humans spent a month on a 1000-piece jigsaw puzzle only to find the last piece missing. It was later discovered in my bed all chewed up!"
Wolfy, age 12

CAT CONFESSIONS

"Nobody knows how a set of muddy paw prints appeared on the art homework my human was due to present at school. She probably won't be leaving her things out on the table again though!" **Mog, age 10**

"I'm not supposed to bring mice indoors to play with!" **Rex, age 8**

"I accidentally slipped and fell into the bathtub whilst Daddy was having a relaxing bubble bath! Unfortunately, the traumatic moments which followed during my evacuation resulted with him sustaining several lacerations to various body parts, some quite delicate! I didn't mean it; I'd never heard Daddy scream before!" **Mittens, age 2**

"I'm no longer allowed to share mealtimes with my sibling after the vet discovered she's lost 1 kilo whereas I've gained nearly two!" **Bobby, age 5**

CAT CONFESSIONS

"My Human's hand is not a chew toy, and his arm is also not a scratch post!"   **Furball, age 1**

"I wasn't Supposed to take Daddy's slipper through the cat flap and leave it out in the garden all night when it started to rain!"   **Moose, age 9**

"I must stop confusing Daddy by pretending Mummy hasn't fed me breakfast yet when he wakes up!"   **Nacho, age 4**

"Running in between Daddy's legs as he made his way down the stairs was very silly of me! Luckily, it was only a hairline fracture to the ankle that he suffered, and just a small dent in the wall!"   **Clawdia, age 5**

"Bringing and releasing a live bird into the room where Mummy was chairing a virtual meeting on her work laptop was extremely unprofessional of me!" **Gizmo, age 13**

CAT CONFESSIONS

"Turns out the goldfish doesn't move quite so elegantly when removed from the aquarium whereas Mummy becomes extraordinarily quick and agile!" Meg, age 8

"I'm supposed to eat directly from my food bowl, I'm not supposed to pick the food out and eat from the floor every time!" Barnaby, age 4

"The fact the fire-brigade now know me by name after I've been stuck up the same tree on three separate occasions is not something to be proud of!" Spud, age 9

"Greeting Daddy at work when he opened the back doors on his van to get his tools out after having arrived at his clients home didn't go down as well as I had hoped!" Fifi, age 7

CAT CONFESSIONS

"Leaving my butt hanging over the edge of my litter tray Is not how it's supposed to work!" Panther, age 11

"My human's thigh is not meant to be my own personal footrest when I'm relaxing on the sofa!" Tilly, age 5

"Kneading on Mummy's new expensive dress to create a cosy spot to take a nap on is not acceptable! Even though she did leave it laid out across the bed whilst she took a shower!" Taco, age 17

"Rugby tackling Daddy's legs when he got up to go to the toilet in the middle of the night when it was pitch-black was inappropriate! I was only playing; I didn't realise he couldn't see!" Pistachio, age 3

CAT CONFESSIONS

"It's not very neighbourly to sit on the external windowsill of next door's dining room and stare directly at them through the window without blinking whilst they eat their breakfast every morning!" Chop Suey, age 9

"I got caught going through the cat flap next door to eat their cat's food!" Stormy, age 5

"Mummy's hooped earring was not supposed to be a new cat toy for me! I didn't realise ears could bleed that much!" Malibu, age 1

"The bonnet on Daddy's Mercedes after he's just pulled into our driveway is not my very own personal heated seat!" Bertha, age 13

"I knocked a vase of the table and tried to make it seem like the dog had done it when Daddy came to see what the loud smash was!" Kitten, age 4

CAT CONFESSIONS

"I sneaked into next door's kitchen and took their string of sausages from the counter. Unfortunately, they saw me running back to my garden with the sausages dragging along the ground behind me! They told my mummy what I did, and she was very angry with me and had to apologise to the neighbours and compensate them!"

Snape, age 2

"My human left the scarf she was knitting on the armchair one night. The following morning the soft ball of wool had been unravelled, chewed through, and was all over the living room floor! It's remained a mystery, nobody knows how it happened!"

Skittles, age 4

"I tried climbing up the chimney which resulted in me becoming incredibly dirty and dusty. Afterwards, I casually walked around the house for a bit, before settling down for a nice nap on the sofa! When my humans returned home in the evening, they weren't very pleased with what they found!"

Whiskers, age 5

"The pile of freshly ironed laundry is not a cat bed!"

Nugget, age 12

Amazing facts about cats:

- Cats can jump up to 6 times their own height.

- Cats spend around 13 to 16 hours per day sleeping.

- A domestic cat shares 95.6% of its genetic makeup with a tiger.

- The oldest recorded cat to have ever lived was called Creme Puff who was 38 years and 3 days old when he passed away (1967 – 2005).

- When a cat rubs against you, it's not just a sign of affection! They're also using their scent glands to mark you as their territory to basically tell other cats that you are their property!

- It's believed that a cat's purr isn't just a sign of being content, the vibrations can actually help them deal with stress, illness and heal injuries.

- Cats are crepuscular meaning they are mostly active around dusk and dawn.

- Male cats are more likely to be left-pawed, whereas female cats are more likely to be right-pawed.

- When your cat looks at you and slowly blinks, it's telling you it feels safe, comfortable, and that it loves you.

- Ever noticed your cat opening their mouth when sniffing something. This is called taste-scenting, they have an extra organ allowing them to taste the scent in the air.

- Kittens from the same litter can have different fathers.

- The average domesticated cat can run around 30 mph (48 kph).

- Studies reveal that living with a cat is beneficial for your health and wellbeing

Amazing facts about cats:

- A cat can see around 6 times better than a human at night.

- Studies have shown that the more you talk to your cat, the more it will talk to you! So, if your cat is particularly chatty, we know it's highly likely that you spend a lot of your free time talking to it!

- Out of all mammals, cats have the largest eyes relative to the size of their heads.

- Cats have over 100 different types of vocalisations to communicate, whereas dogs have around 10.

- It's believed that meowing is a behaviour that cats developed so that they could communicate with humans.

- A cat's ability to learn new things is at a similar level to a 2- to 3-year-old child.

- Research shows that cats are able to sense the emotions of their human and detect when you're happy, sad, or anxious. It's believed they develop this over time by analysing your facial structure as well as sensing changes in the tone of your voice depending on how you're feeling. This is the reason they can't detect different emotions in strangers!

- Cats can adapt their meow to manipulate you! Yes, remember earlier when you gave your cat a treat because it looked at you with those big, cute eyes and kept meowing? It was actually all premediated by your fluffy dictator!

- No matter how naughty your cat is, it's impossible to ever be angry with them because they instinctively know how to instantly look cute and innocent! Okay, this last fact is made-up, but we think it's definitely true!

A big thank you to everyone who has purchased this book!

My furry co-author and I hope you've enjoyed reading this book as much as we loved creating it. I hope its raised a few smiles and chuckles along the way, or perhaps reassured you that your own little furball, past or present; is in good company with all the other purrrfectly cheeky cats out there!

Rest assured, whoever you are, wherever you are, you're not alone in the never-ending quest to try and get your cat to simply, behave! As you can see, I can personally vouch for that!

Printed in Great Britain
by Amazon

32123698R00059